Palace of Twigs

poems by

Diana Deering

Finishing Line Press
Georgetown, Kentucky

Palace of Twigs

Copyright © 2022 by Diana Deering
ISBN 979-8-88838-005-5 First Edition
All rights reserved under International and Pan-American Copyright Conventions. No part of this book may be reproduced in any manner whatsoever without written permission from the publisher, except in the case of brief quotations embodied in critical articles and reviews.

Publisher: Leah Huete de Maines
Editor: Christen Kincaid
Cover Art: Bridget Fischer
Author Photo: Susan Burgers
Cover Design: Elizabeth Maines McCleavy

Order online: www.finishinglinepress.com
also available on amazon.com

Author inquiries and mail orders:
Finishing Line Press
P. O. Box 1626
Georgetown, Kentucky 40324
U. S. A.

Table of Contents

1. Insomnia
2. Time and Chance, After Holes Punched in Our Beings
3. As a Child
4. I Sketch the Resin-Weed
5. After Hearing a Mycologist
6. The End of Winter
7. Standing Close to the Great Change We Call Death
8. Snail
9. When She Told Me
10. Hospital Rounds with my Father
11. In This World But Not Of It
12. The Spiritual Life of Ants
13. Photosynthesis
14. Los Angeles
15. Ice Skater
16. Saltines
17. The Devotion of Objects
18. The Last Vacant Lot
19. In a Child's Day, There is a Keyhole To Heaven
20. Sweet Tooth
21. Steal
22. Desiderata
23. Where Does the Music Come From?
24. Palace of Twigs
25. Mole
26. Ode to the Sow Bug
27. Ode to the Cabbage
28. After Backpacking
29. Up Here We Are Scissored Birds
30. Wildflowers
31. September Morning
32. You Died on the First Day of Spring
33. My Mother's Loneliness
34. No Mustard Seed
35. Assisted Living
36. When My Mother Died

37. A Changed State
39. After a Night Shift at the Hospice
40. The Monk & the Cookies
41. While Hiking on Cascade Pass I Forgive My Own Hunger
42. Lifting the Split-Leaf Philodendron
43. The Single White Rose

Palace of Twigs

Insomnia

Like a sheet shook out hard,
wings bore up from the beach at 2:49 a.m.

Then a keening,
motherless and wild-eyed.

My heart hangs earthbound in its cage,
sways slightly, weary of the surge

from fuses and small fires
smoldering upstream.

I would close the door for my animal
so she could sleep without burning.

Time and Chance
After Holes Punched In Our Beings

That summer the fruit trees were laden,
green apples brushed with red,

Babies slipped out of their mothers
at nine months or a few weeks early.

Creamy unbroken skin, all ten toes intact,
I was privately relieved.

The days were cool, we slept in,
made kind gestures, restored to a childhood concern for order.

I thought the downward slide might have broken,
when we watched little girls run shrieking into the waves

and did not mourn for ourselves.

As a Child

I wandered the canyon behind our house,
animal trails carved the hillsides
the kids skidded down.
There were scrub oaks, sage,
poppies briefly in spring,
clumps of grass flattened
by rabbits and night coyotes.
I gathered leaves, fallen sticks,
speckled granite for my pockets.
At dusk, I climbed the thin path to our house,
closed the door to my room, and for hours
bent to the small lucid things,
arranging and re-arranging
their shapes before the lamp.

I sketch the resin-weed

I sketch the resin-weed with my untrained eye,

 a pencil borrowed from your father,

like missing someone before you have met,

the taste of them is that strong.

I want to stay true to the form, three caplets per stem,

striated cup, solid rim. I love how they materialize

everywhere, weedy and delicate, as a girl who stood out

silvery and plain, see-through, right down to her veins.

After Hearing a Mycologist Speak about the Subterranean Mycelial Plate

Overnight,
through pine needles
and lime green moss,
mushrooms lift
like small strange trees.

Copper and ivory,
phosphorescent red,
boletes, amanita rubescens,
fairy rings.

Underground,
filaments weave vast
sensate mats,
spanning whole continents,
unknown except for the brief
thrust of fruit.

A squirrel tears
a spongy tap from its stem
exposes the delicate underneath
wheel of radiating blades,
gills like the layered
throats of trout.

A centipede crosses
the mantle of earth,
its hundred feet
like small soundless brushes.

The End of Winter
thinking of Linda

She had not eaten for days, pain a brand under the skin,
a north-wind burning under every door.

She bequeaths her horse to an island neighbor,
her dogs wander glassy eyed through the house.

Carefully I lift her head to free the throat, the fold of ear,
trace pale eyelids with a warm cloth.

All day the leaves were particled air, almost liquid,
pressed in close to the car as I drove

on back roads from house to house,
their threaded ribs steam see-through

in the brief sun between rains.
I rolled down the windows to breathe their green exhale.

Standing Close to the Great Change We Call Death

He lies under a red blanket in a house beneath cedars
His wife reminds me of my mother
Envelopes with careful return addresses wait by the door

She offers coffee, arranges his meds on a tray in the crowded kitchen
Plays Brahms now that he cannot speak
I kneel beside his bed and see that already

his eyes are lighted from the back with the light
I've seen enter through the seams of barns
slice through prairie grass

When I leave it is almost dark
deer gather beside fences
I long for them like a mother or sister

When they turn all at once
I would follow them into the hollows
to fold down in the leaves to rest

All night they slip past the houses
I hear the thump of their hooves
Daily I study the inner sleeve they inhabit

How do they walk inside
the cups of their eyes without moving?
What do they listen to?

Snail

Exhausted,
I pace long hallways
out the hospital door at midnight.
A snail is crossing the sidewalk.
Its transparent horns reflect the moon,
the liquid trail of its melting body glistens.
I pull my coat around my shoulders,
stopped before its slow determined passage
under a cold sky.
How brave and complicated it is to be alive.

What She Told Me

Across the passage, the dark shape of a whale
moves just beneath grey water, the curve of its back
surfaces then rolls underneath, as if entering
a world of dreaming. The seasons thin at both edges,
the way an exhaled breath disappears
into a cave of darkness before the long turn upward.

Yesterday she told me that in the ambulance,\
as she struggled to breathe, in that moment being wholly
animal, submerged, as she paused between worlds,
before rounding the corner back into this one,
her mother appeared to her in a familiar white dress
and said: "Whatever happens you will be okay."

I thanked her, stood up to go. As I stepped
into the five o'clock air, my legs were buoyant,
almost weightless, like falling and being caught.
The way behind the sky the pattern of stars
is already shining, years before they sent out their light,
they have always known this.

Hospital Rounds with my Father, Age Seven

Through the whoosh of the double doors,
past the gift shop, along the shiny floors to the back halls,
his large hand held mine.

The elevator crowded with patients rolled in on gurneys,
we stood still, pressed into the back.

As we lifted with a jolt,
I would sneak a look at their faces.
Their eyes were glassy and shaken

like stunned birds fallen
back from our living room window.

Those nights the leaves of my lungs
bloomed between my collar bones and scapula
with a grainy inarticulate ache.

I placed the birds' hollow weight in shoeboxes
lined with torn nightgowns and a thimble of water.

My best friend
had a hole in her heart,
her lips turned purple at recess.

Ants circled under the benches, solemnly dragging
their injured on pine needles and dried pieces of grass.

In This World but Not of It

The priest said when I was ten in the wooden pew
beside my best friend's mother.

We watched her spread Rose Milk
on her arms as she dressed for Mass.

I felt the hard muscles of my thighs climb over live oak trails,
rest among umbels of cow parsnip where moths dusted their feet.

When she had the seizure in the grocery aisle
between the bread and crates of fruit,

before she fell, did she see the light blue foreheads
of schoolchildren clasping candy bars,

the radiance of lemons.
Did she feel heat

rise off the butcher's hands
as he held her shoulders,

eased her down to the floor.

The Spiritual Life of Ants

My father saved my life once
when as an infant I slipped under the bath water.
My mother found me motionless and floating,
he lifted me and gave me mouth to mouth.

I learned secrets the way ants build colonies in darkness
under the skin of blacktop, how they rise
to swarm above ground in moving brown bands,
grind beaded sand to flour.

In the catacombs they massage each other's abdomens
to expel a single drop of syrup for the queen.
The world keeps saving me, lifting me out,
each day another link, another bridge back.

Photosynthesis

As a child walking at dusk I looked into the windows,
pulled to the light of each lamp, the women I could see moving in kitchens.

Yellow light seeped onto lawns,
suffused the luminous houses.

I became a child of subterfuge,
practiced at the subtle art of being

in the presence of the beloved
without any visible signs of wanting.

Tiptoeing in, my body slipped into bed next to my mother.
The weight of her breasts grazed my side,

through her nightgown her skin was the sun.
I drew her heat across my borders,

the way a leaf catches light in its mesh glove,
absorbs the complex chains

and rainbow prism
for the later work.

Still under my skin the nocturnal cells clatter,
disturbing my sleep.

Always one ear cocked to the manufacture and harvest,
the labor for the simple sugars.

Los Angeles, 1962

On the 405, to the 605, to the 5,
the Plymouth station wagon swings onto onramps and overpasses,

rocks like a boat in the watery dark of Pirates of the Caribbean.
I play stewardess in the back seat, the seatbelt's buckle my microphone.

Fasten your seatbelts please, No smoking please,
I chime over and over, as my sister stares out the window.

We drift, planets spun loose from their sun,
randomly colliding over the white vinyl seats.

I could be sucked out of the back seat, float
in front of the windshield, like a dress.

I have seen babies in incubators under the warming lights,
nurses bend down to cup the pulsing fontanels.

I became adept at self- warming,
the way insects wait to twirl out of their casings,

open the pleats of their wings one by one when no one is looking,
but quickly though or one could die from the cold.

Ice Skater

Your skates cut a sharp calligraphy
leave a light waterless powder in their wake.

I watch from under the ice,
the way fish might look up at sky in winter,

learn to tell time by the movement of shadows
and the blocked out sun.

Your voice catches in my ears,
a dark hook I cannot escape.

I make pacts,
move my socks from the bottom drawer,

fold my underwear carefully,
stop speaking at dinner,

I grow colorless, wary,

listen for the garage door to open
when you return late from the hospital,

hear you drop your keys in the turquoise dish,
step out of your shoes.

Automatically, without knowing,
the way the spinal fluid of fish

adjusts to changes in temperature,
I skim the dark floor, adopt the faraway pulse of sleep.

By day at the skating rink,
you glide us in long strides over the ice.

Others watch in amazement
as you scrape to a stop on a dime.

Saltines

We slide into a booth near the window, my dad and me,
 my tailbone brushes the damp vinyl seat.

Waitresses in checkered aprons move with an undersea weariness,
their eyelids heavy as fish hanging in torpor.

I concentrate, will myself up, against the weight of air-conditioning
and lifetimes of water, to surface to table, fork and spoon,

saltines in cellophane packages,
fanned edges like gills.

Crispy squares to place on my tongue,
light filled tunnels of air and salt.

The Devotion of Objects

To emerge into air,
to cereal boxes and the logic of spoons,

bliss to crawl under tables
swish beneath dresses.

Even the see through cross hatching of envelopes
that wait on my mother's desk,

when held up to light,
each almost invisible fiber

holds together
for just this purpose,

to carry letters and
the beauty of stamps.

The Last Vacant Lot

High above the houses, in the makeshift baseball diamond,
my shoulders shake a little, a bird combing its continents,

the scoured southern California plain riveted to its corners.
I map the reservoir and Ford dealership,

the cemetery where they put out poisoned hamburger
for the tomcat. The library and Wisteria bakery,

where lemon sheet cakes wait in lighted cases.
Fathers dress for offices,

cars pulled by underground magnets angle into driveways.
Parents play bridge on card tables,

keep score on flowered tablets.
The air is thick, almost impassable,

children under heavy aprons
spit into porcelain bowls,

goldfish slide under bridges,
streetlights continue their slow motion

harmonic that is not mine,
but I am not a stranger to it.

In my twin bed under the window
the crickets throb bores in.

In a Child's Day, There is a Keyhole to Heaven

I floated above my body in a gauzy sleep I could not shake.
It was already hot, the dulled edges of sound came across distances,

a plane droned overhead, the voice of my mother.
I paced like a sleepwalker, my feet pulled in their white net.

Somewhere children were getting haircuts, being dropped off at swim class,
women pored through binders of Butterick and Simplicity,

pinned brown onion skin patterns along dotted lines.
I pressed through heavy air, submerged in a spell I could not break.

When my foot caught a chipped sweet gum leaf, suddenly
a world revealed.

When held up to light, each vein a snaking river, darkened nuclei,
threaded spindles I learned about in fourth grade.

Its skin gave off a sequestered light, the way a star harnesses a used up
sun in its five points, until it is self luminous.

Sweet Tooth

We lined up behind the bakery truck,
as he pulled out drawers of glistening doughnuts.

Each sugary ring tucked in wax paper,
from his money belt he clicked out quarters for change.

The ice cream man's jingle sent us racing outside,
squawking like chickens

for candy cigarettes,
popsicles that stained our lips crimson.

In the top drawer of my dresser
I arranged tubes of pixie sticks,

Columns of sweet-tarts and smarties in neat rows,
to last until my next allowance.

I divvied them out,
disciplined as a cold eyed pragmatist,

a banker monitoring her assets,
until that first taste of sour cherry hung in my mouth,

and I spun out,
lost in a cloud of addled ecstasy.

Steal

A friend tried to teach me to shoplift,
expertly gleaning her haul

beneath roving salespeople
and one-way mirrors,

progressing from mascara at the corner pharmacy
to lingerie at I. Magnin's within months.

I could never shake my terror of being
handcuffed, thrown behind bars.

When her father left,
her mother went bankrupt.

Her spoils were evidence of prowess,
finesse, the thrill of the prize.

I settled for salvage, prayed for transcendence,
before acne scrubs and foundations,

repeating the names of eyeshadows:
smoky teal, café au lait, crushed velvet,

like a pilgrim at Lourdes. With coins
I stole from my father's piggyback,

I laid down my burden before the cashier.

Desiderata

You are a child of the universe

the poster declared in my friend's living room.
She had four Siamese cats,
her father played trumpet in LA.nightclubs.

Beside their low leather couch, LP's spun,
'Mama may have, papa may have, but God bless the child...'

Sunday mornings as her family ate crepes with jam and strong coffee,
I slipped away to stand before the good news,

turned my body toward its promise
like a novice mouthing the words.

No less than the trees and the stars
You have a right to be here.

We dabbed L'Air de Temps behind our ears,
practiced tongue kisses, ran to dive under ten foot waves.

Girl-women, we were on fire,
thrilled to the pleasure of our bodies.

Her mother gave me The Diary of Anais Nin
for my fourteenth birthday.

She told her daughter to choose carefully
with whom she first made love,

that for a woman, this first
was a complicated and holy flowering.

Where Does the Music Come From

A poem infuses the hands that hold the book,
steeps the skin of fingers, as Darjeeling

leaves darken a waiting cup of water.
Sound travels through oceans, vibrations

clock ten thousand miles between whales
to unlock the childhood ear.

Where does the music come from she asks?
Where does it go when its over?

The swallows are wheeling for insects, they tumble inside octaves of air,
defying gravity, they steer into culverts,

sip mid-flight and are gone. Even I who wanted to fly,
could hardly stay down, put rocks in my shoes to remember

that I was not only longing, but was becoming visible,
inevitable, the way one glimpses one's sister

in a crowd by the gestural slant of her head,
her carriage, the shape of her mouth.

Palace of Twigs

The stem of my body lengthens,
pulled like filings to a magnet's edge.
I float, see-through,

bump blindly as a moth,
still the perfect distance of things
opens in the ladder of branches.

A wood rat's palace of twigs,
sedge and the scaled spears of horsetail,
scouring rush, ancient Equisetum's black tipped spears.

I weave through thickets of salal,
sarcococca, wax white snowberry.
The alder's four-fingered catkins dangle,

swing lightly as bracelets.
The ground is saturated, almost purple brown,
earth-slick skin,

leaves melt from fluted bones,
among the beetle's rasp
and dark bottles of root.

Mole

A mole searches for auguries in the dark,
exhumes subterranean watchtowers, roots the ancient record of trees.

Beneath muffled footsteps of badger and humans, the strange roll of cars,
their expert hands expose cellars of earthworms

who coil and uncoil in slow motion communion with the earth.
This darkness is elemental work I tell it,

to propel in a tunnel of one's own making
with only the click of insects for company.

Spiders construct their meticulous wheels,
beetles chisel into rock, without lamps or the benefit of stars.

I believe in the mole and its gods,
even now, especially in winter.

Ode to the Sow Bug

You burrow
in the corky bark
of logs I bring in
for the stove.
Steel gray helmets,
crustaceans
from the Cambrian
fossil record,
roly poly,
survivor of ice ages
& human epochs,

Under your armor
your body
curls out of sight.
Your twin antennae,
two back paddles,
& fourteen jointed limbs
fold in like oars of a outrigger
arched in its own sea.

Traveler between worlds,
wood spirit,
your script curlicues
across alder and fir,
inlaid in moss and lime-green
wolf lichen,
you fall to the floor
like a grain of rice.

Ode to the Cabbage

You have seen women huddle in kitchens,
You have seen famine,
Heard horse hooves pound their iron warning.
Plagues in Bellie Parish, Morayshire, Scotland
where my father's ancestors were shopkeepers.

All winter you wait,
tough as bowling balls in fog-shrouded fields,
jade green globes protect a central fist,
an infant's head birthed
crown first.

You have borne witness,
Given over to boiling pots, knives and spoons,
Steamed to translucent sweetness,
You have soothed children and old men,
You have fed the masses,

Brassica cruciferae,
Miraculous.

After Backpacking

As we speed down the interstate on a hot August evening,
the scent of plants thickens the air.
First sage, then fennel, and the drying grasses.

We have lived for five days in the mountains,
slept beside rivers, and a high blue lake,
among alpine flowers.

Shooting stars, Fairy lanterns,
yellow throats of corn lilies,
the high pitched call of a Townsend's Solitaire.

Now as darkness veils the summer hills,
beside the highway a cow lumbers on its path,
her tail a dark braid.

For a moment I know her life,
sure of nothing, walking on and on
over the wide answering earth.

Up Here We Are Scissored Birds

Half returned to shale and mountain goat, we have crossed ridges,
touched the undersides of morels and fern's dotted braille.

Glaciers hold their silences.
I go toward their constant light to be buried or held.

Ravens chortle and whirl upside down,
above downy oat grass meadows at 6,000 feet.

Wind pours through firs lining the Elwha valley,
blueberries fire from orange to red.

We rest in a field of spent pasque flowers, fallen lily stalks,
white spokes liquefied by frost.

Each remaining upright stem singular, honed to cylinder and ellipsis,
beaded rattles, insect spines frozen in rock.

Wildflowers

It's not that we couldn't count them,

Bistort, Valerian, Silene,
to hear the names in the mouth.

Saw-wort, Arnica, Birdbeak,
to call ourselves rich,

matching the field guide's descriptions,
basal-leafed, sheathed, elliptical.

But that night in the floating before sleep,
I drown in the Nooksack's roar,

destroying all tallies.

September Morning

The air is distilled, mineral,
close to the ground, damp as matted leaves.

Flat stars of queen anne's lace and bristles of fireweed gone to seed.
The grasses sound hollow now, electric, light and quick as an insect's carapace.

I find silver-bloodied fur the owl dropped last night,
hind leg of a rabbit, suede taut as my father's fraying moccasins.

A deer lifts her head, eyes dark ponds, rinsed and mirror-like after rain.
We stand there unblinking. She looks through me and steadily beyond,

the way a dying person
unfastened, gazes into the next world.

You Died on the First Day of Spring

Flying north, the plane glides over Sierra snowfields,
lakes are clouded mirrors ringed in ice,

a frozen expanse without roads or humans
like grief.

You were remote as these dotted caves,
animals raised to survive all manner of cold,

who store loneliness beneath wool coats, kindle
small bonfires of manufactured cellular heat.

You skated to school all winter in Glengarry County,
northern Ontario, slotted right forward in matches

with country boys on backwoods ponds,
secured center at Queens and McGill.

You pumped gas outside your dad's dry goods store,
sung tenor in the church choir,

hauled out cars slid into ditches,
your toes scored with frostbite, burned to get warm.

My Mother's Loneliness

Across the water the darkened windows of summer houses
are saturated like caves.

The calmness of clouds come for me,
their millions of droplets and broken corners of rocks and flowers lift.

All day I include my body,
see again the edges of leaves.

Husbandless, you carry his ashes up
three flights to your apartment, surprised by their weight.

Sentient osteoclasts, leg bones porous with air,
pumice cliffs holed with swallows.

You move alone in your rooms,
bared now to the sea.

No Mustard Seed

Rabbits lower their mother of pearl ears, pull in like stone
to an earlier dark of cool passageways dug in hollows underground.

Crows rasp insults, dive from the hot trees,
even they are not immune to brokenness, or a tattered wing to ground them.

Stunned by the heat, one bird turns in slow circles beside the highway,
cranes its beak upward for air.

Carrying her dead child, Kisa Gotami went door to door
in search of a house untouched by grief.

You ask me: Did I do okay, was I a good mother?
Shards of glass can fly up unexpectedly in a sudden wind.

I want to protect the fluid oceans of my eyes,
what they can see from here.

Assisted Living

Pharmacy supplies arrive, churchgoers board the facility bus,
a dryness in my eyes unaccustomed to the too bright sun.

Aristotle said the soul thinks in pictures.
I composed scenes I could wish myself into,

then arms had the sensitivity of branches, fingers were root tips,
yellow lamps waited in corner windows,

boxes of pens and paperclips
on the counter of the Five and Dime.

The bone plates of my mother's face are becoming visible,
bound on an underground river,

she and I swift past ice floes
and caverns that receive no light,

crystalline pools, magnificent fish never to be known.
We have our small pacts.

I say good night, touch her shoulder,
fold down her covers, weep a little before I sleep.

When My Mother Died

When my mother died, I wondered if something
insatiable in me would quiet, an object of longing
finally out of reach.

A long overseas voyage, suitcase dangling,
a continuous embarrassment,
like a torn hem or a begging bowl.

The monotone, morning, noon, night
squinting toward land, a distant
snow-capped peak, shrouded in mist.

Years of preparation on smaller slopes, attempting
to master the hand holds, carabiners, ice picks, ropes,
special light shoes required to stay abreast.

I remember at nine, screwing up my courage,
as I rehearsed in the next room, waiting
for the opportunity to tell her that I loved her.

As soon as I made my entrance, I knew
my project was doomed—she brushed me off,
otherwise occupied, recoiling from my weighty affection.

Now my sister and I bend over her hospital bed.
I pour a small amount of warm water
from a cup onto her scalp, a white bead

of shampoo in my palm, make repeated small circles
behind her ears and at the temples with my fingers,
lifting her head to massage the upper neck and occiput.

As though remembering, she closes her eyes,
her mouth falls open as she revels in the touch,
exhausted, hungry as a child.

A Changed State

> *Energy is neither created nor destroyed, it only changes states*
> (Einstein's 1st Law of Thermodynamics)

As daughters do, in the days, weeks, months
following, I move in a kind of trance, enact unexplained rituals,

arrange and re-arrange objects on coffee tables, order my closets
by color and pattern pleasing to the eye, as though swept

forward in a pre-ordained sequence that events have made surface.
Like the robins, who descend now by the hundreds,

stream into the hawthorn to pluck
the last berries before the longest night of the year,

one ear cocked to the ground, bound to an inner listening.
I peer into faded photographs from the 30's and 40's

severe-faced Methodists buttoned up to their necks,
braced against another Eastern winter.

One of you and your sister, bows in your hair,
kicking your legs out from a high bench swing

in a rare moment of abandon.
I stand before a quartet of your favorite drawings

now hung in my hallway where I pass them
as you did, numberless times a day.

A Degas study in pencil of dancers unlacing their pointe shoes;
 a pen and ink of a village street in Barbizon,

hand-signed by the artist in 1953, the year of your honeymoon.
You pooled your savings and boarded the Queen Mary in Manhattan,

to cross the Atlantic for a one month European tour,
before you were set to start new jobs out west.

(You recently confided that you couldn't believe
you pulled that off. A month! A rented car motoring switchbacks

through the Alps, Italian lakes, Venice, Rome and blue cove overlooks in
    Monaco.
Paris at night, jazz clubs and every smoky discotheque you could manage).

And the Hiroshige prints that were a wedding gift from your boss, one
of a temple pagoda in snow, women in full ceremonial kimono,

another of a Chinese junk heeling in slanted rain,
its multi-fold sails battened in a convex origami.

I hold my hands up, graze a subtle heat as I pass the frames.

After a Night Shift at the Hospice

Morning, as I walk to my car, two geese pass overhead,
their bugling bounces off the houses,

porch lights glow onto lawns, curtains pulled closed.

I watch the slow motion open and close of their beaks,
wonder if it is you mother,

come back or not yet left, broadcasting alarm.

Along the avenue, cherries are in full bloom.
In another part of the world, cherry blossom viewing,

when families picnic under branches, to watch petals fall like snow,
has been cancelled this year.

We placed ice chips to melt on your tongue,
Susan leaned close to your ear, thanked you for bringing me into the world.

At home I wash my face with the square blue washcloth
I bought ten in a stack for your bed baths,

at the supermarket across the street from your care home,

leaves loosening in October. Sorrow dwells in teeth,
parches the throat. The mothers I made up,

glimpsed in department stores holding their children,

librarians, teachers, the neighbor mom who cut our sandwiches
into perfect triangles, with a bag of chips and two cookies.

I quilted them into me, stitched like padding into the sleeve of a coat,

a buried charm I would touch lightly
at bus-stops and piano lessons, call forth its power.

The Monk & the Cookies

When I saw greed cross the old monk's face
as his hand reached for the last cookie,
something relaxed in me.

Sister, you and I have perched like crows,
to scan the ground, ready to dive
for the first shiny bead,
hunger like a clanking wheel
the guinea pig spun over and over beside our beds,
wearing a hole in the night.

The mother crow whose black wings could block out all light,
whose descending angled sweep
was a dreaded daily occurrence
as we scattered for cover,
she is hungry too,
grandmothers,
aunts and cousins,
transgressing fathers and uncles,
sons, dogs and cats,

The gold fish with milky blue eyes
who flipped itself onto the kitchen floor
hari kari,
rather than live in that house,
the turtle in the plastic tray,
with a palm tree and small dish for water,

its unblinking eyes
and careful yellow feet,
hungry,
one night stepped over the edge.

While Hiking on Cascade Pass
I Forgive My Own Hunger

Next to the trail, a mountain goat calf browses
nose down in valerian, alpine daisy, balsamroot—
so close I can see her eyelashes and two emerging white horns.

The mother bawls from a high ledge, an urgent high-pitched braying,
her head crooked, eyes fixed on the roaming calf
as she propels down the cliff face after it.

A man with a camera moves in close to the young ewe.
I watch from a distance now, ashamed by his unchecked greed
for the perfect shot, for closeness, for beauty

and taking, human craving being boundless,
willing to violate any sacred field.
Is it a thirst

for innocence?
I remember her asking me during that dark time, Are you desperate?
I was. For what could disarm me.

Lifting the Split-Leaf Philodendron

Lifting the split-leaf philodendron to the sink for water
is the ghost of my mother, Saturdays, making the rounds to her plants.

Some believe in a soul signature, embedded in voice or script,
the scrawl of a sentence, gesture of hands, an afterimage that remains in the eye.

My mother's penmanship was tiny,
meticulous as musical notation.

Insects have etched their paths, sawflies and beetles made
skeletons of alder leaves layering the forest floor,

pleated tents half bitten, torn to lace.
I cannot find their bodies anywhere, flown or

burrowed, dissolving
into the next season.

Our toes in snowmelt water, chains of light prism
shadows on river bottom sand,

the Nooksack's sliding turquoise milk.
Mountains scoured, mica grit locked in glacial ice,

140,000 years, epochs,
roll to the sea.

I hold on tightly, my jaw aches, resisting
change. Lately I have imagined water flowing

through my fingers, head-long, unstoppable,
essentially joyous.

I wonder where you are now mother,
among the floating signatures.

The single white rose

The single white rose
left after the dahlia's
edges brown
still breathes,
as if to say only once
we are given bodies
like this to speak.

Diana Deering lives in the Pacific Northwest and works as a hospice nurse. Her chapbook, *Flame Shoulder Moth*, was published by Finishing Line Press.

www.ingramcontent.com/pod-product-compliance
Lightning Source LLC
Chambersburg PA
CBHW030226170426
43194CB00007BA/878